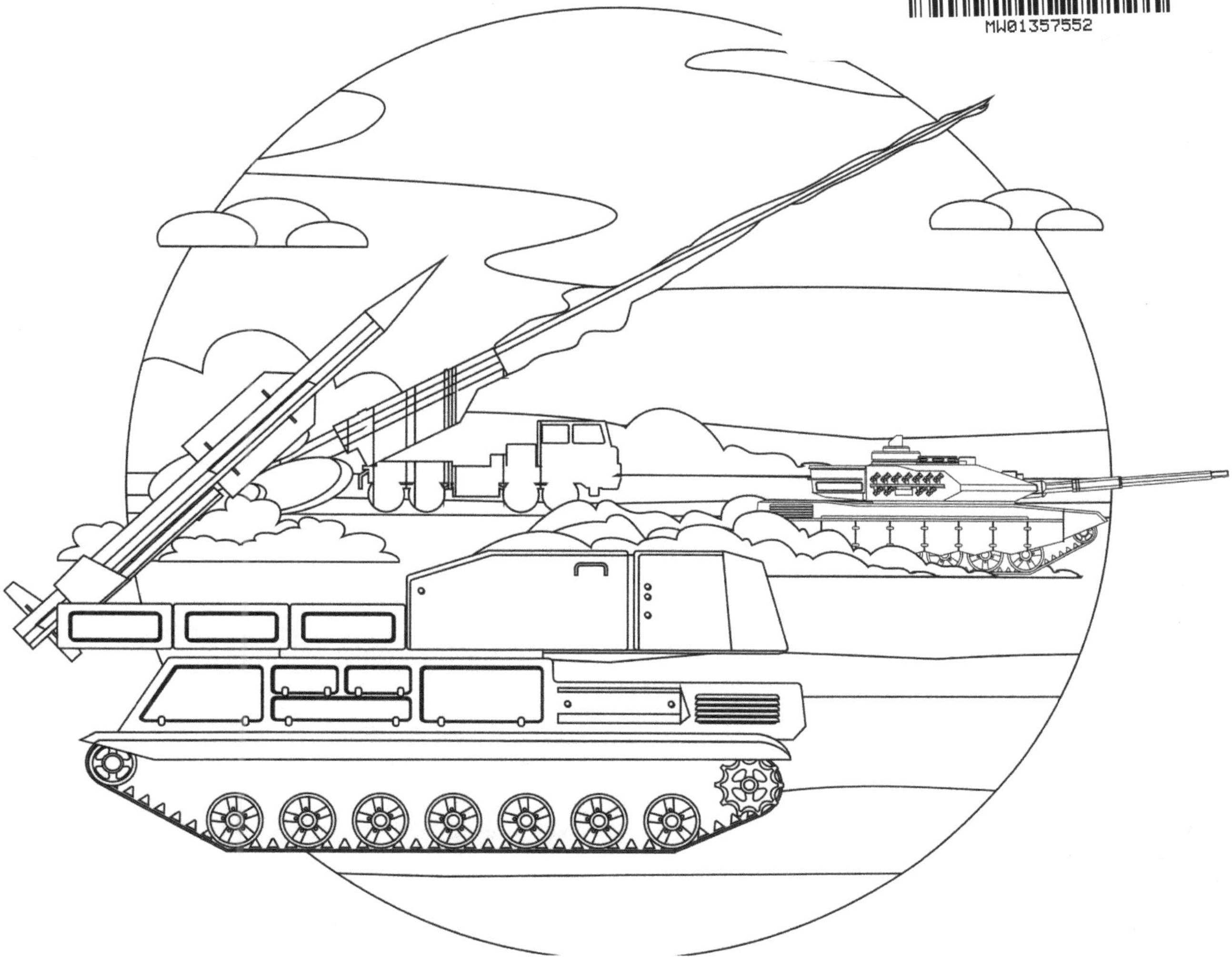

This Book Belongs to

MILITARY BASE

BORDER
CONTROL

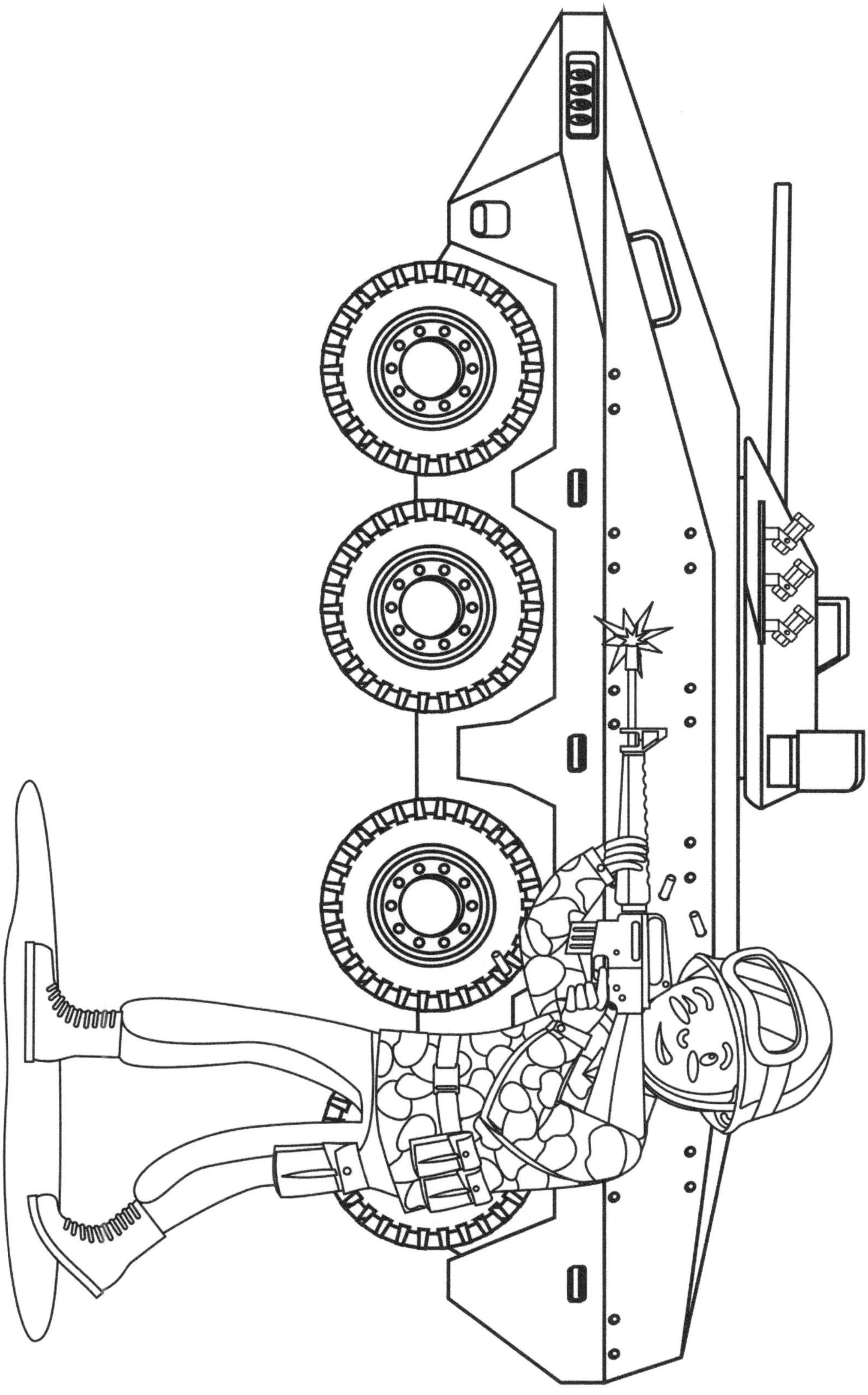

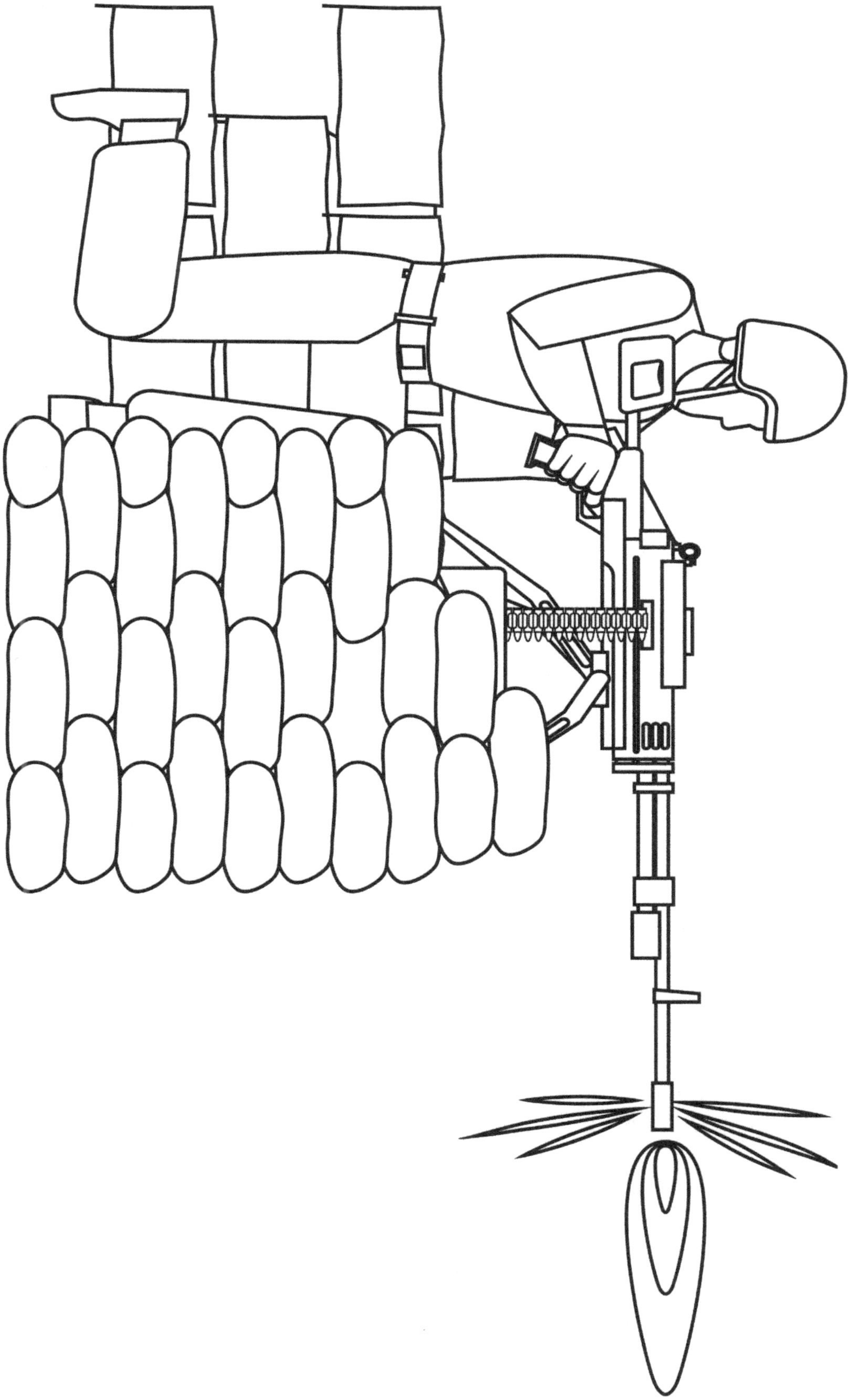

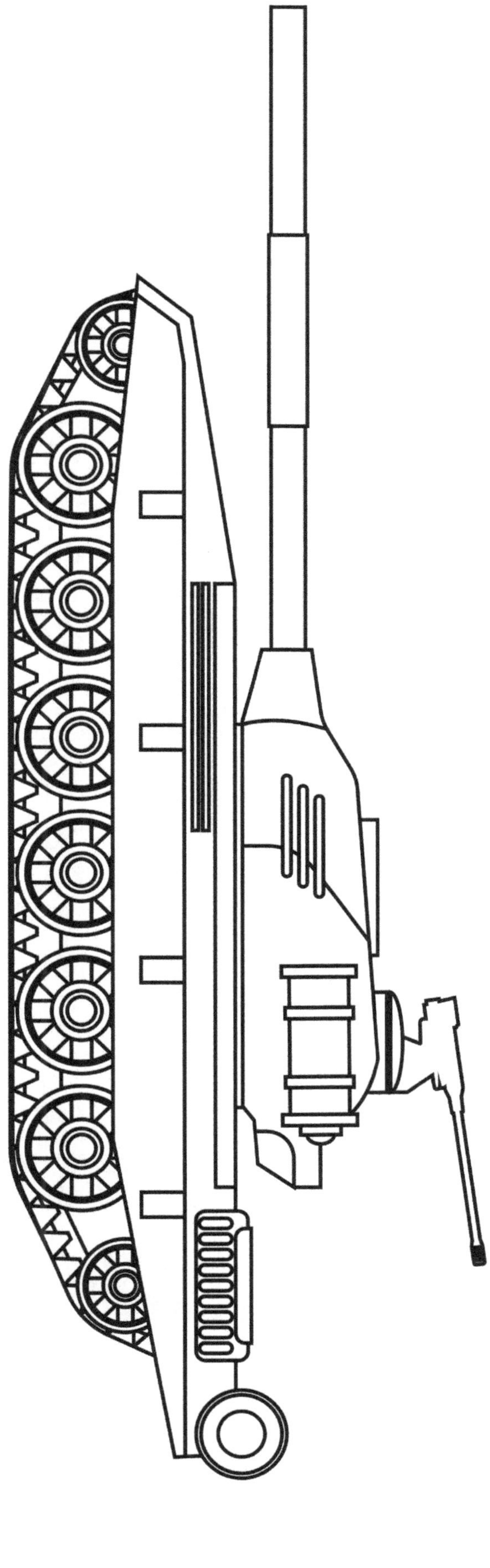

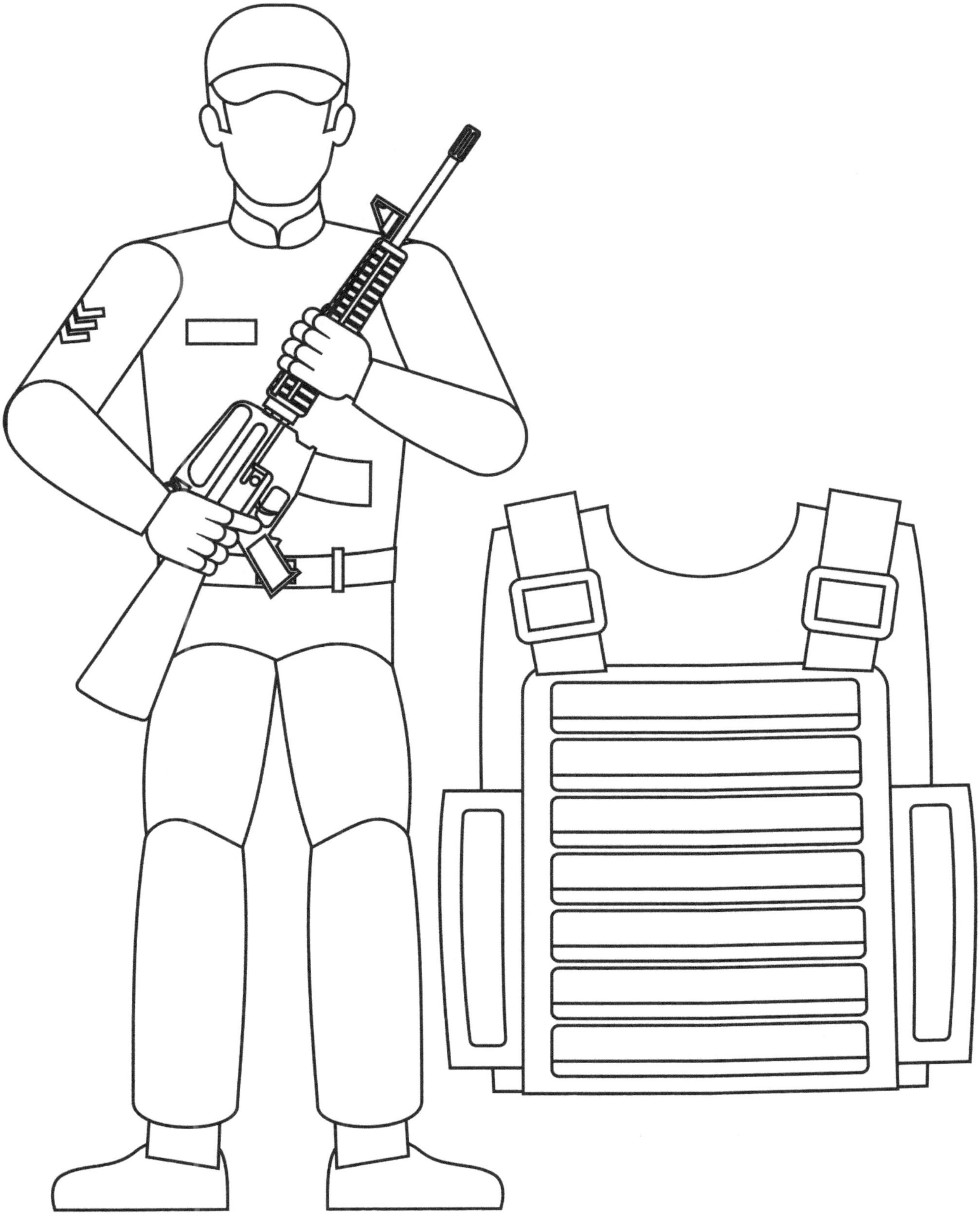

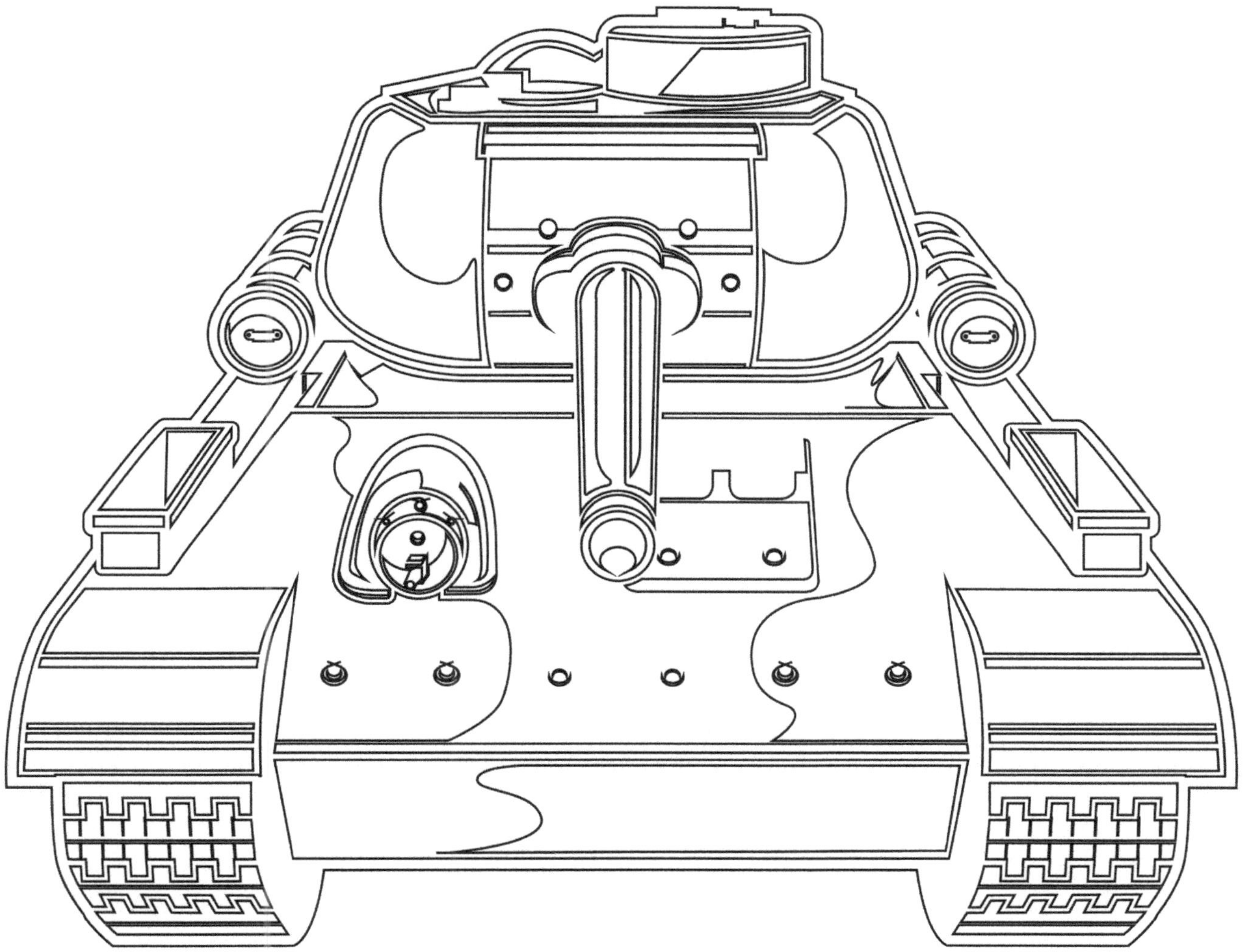

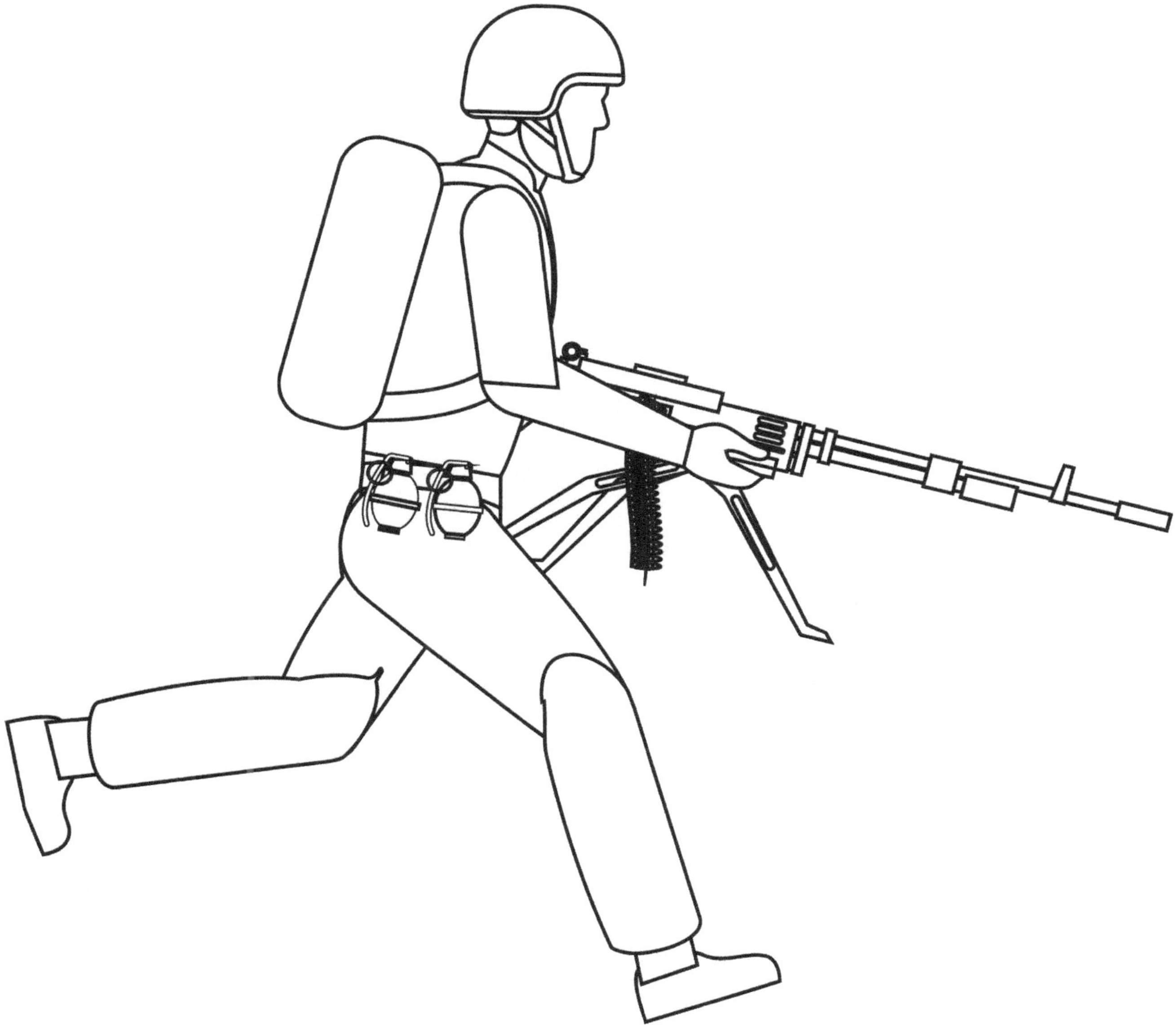

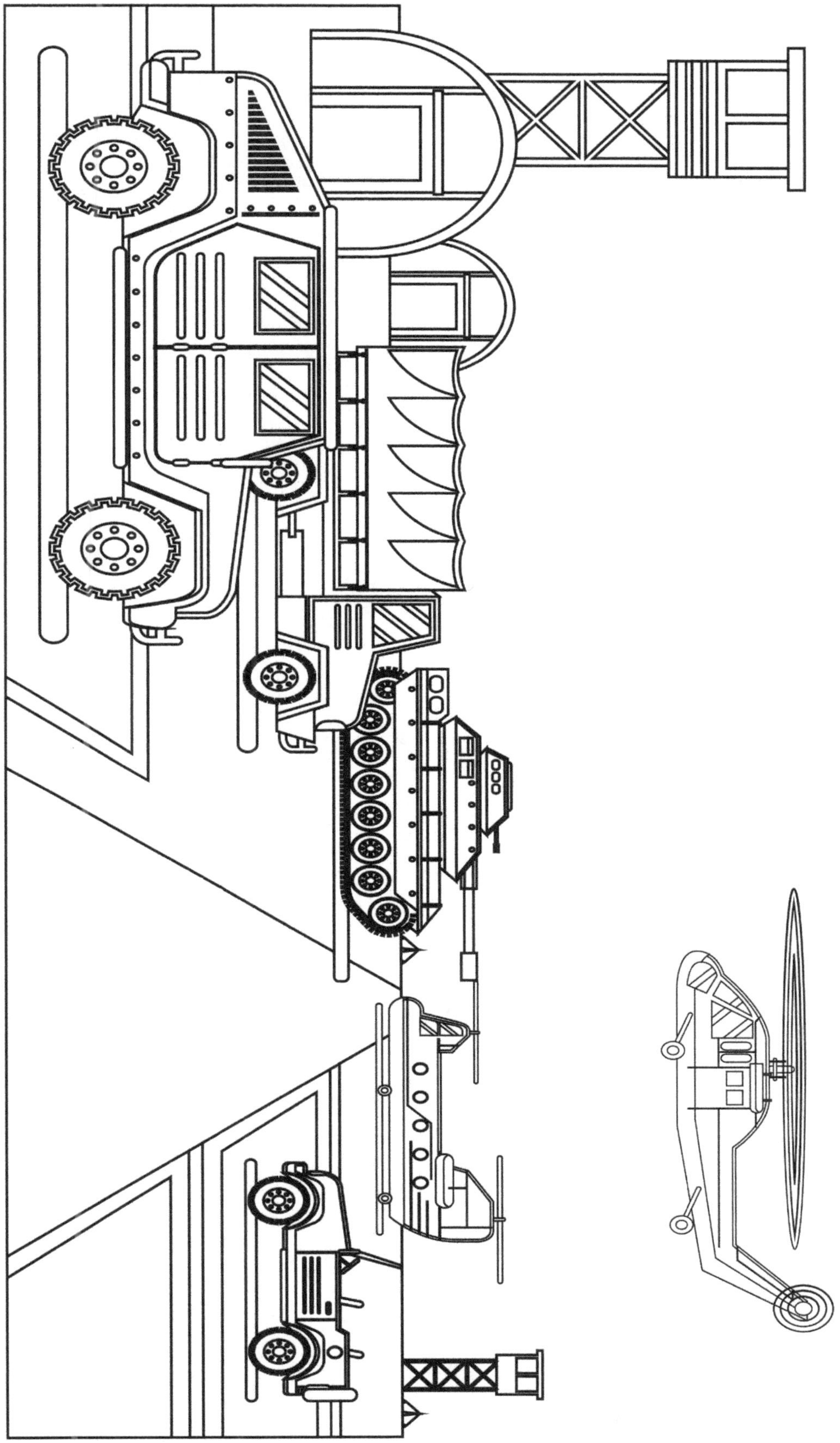

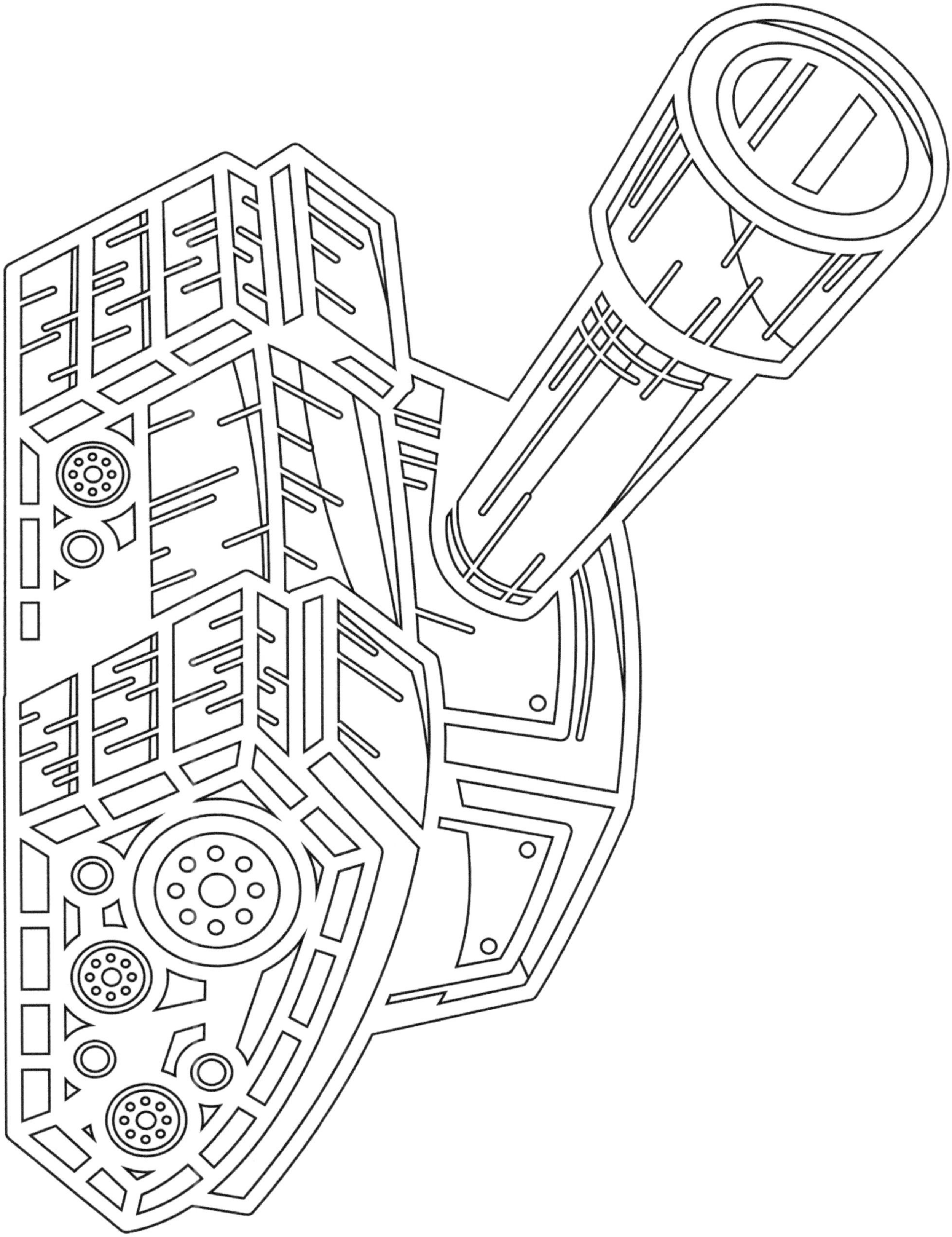

HI

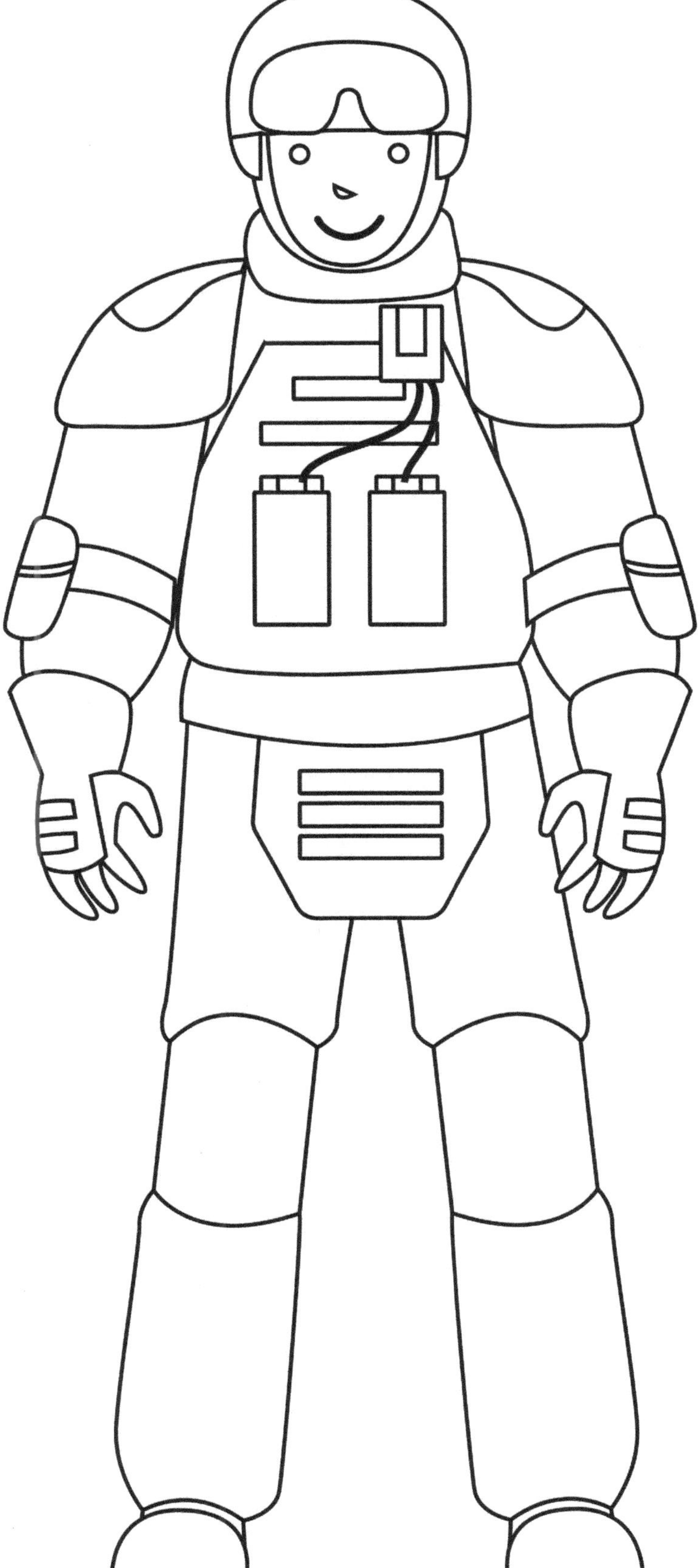

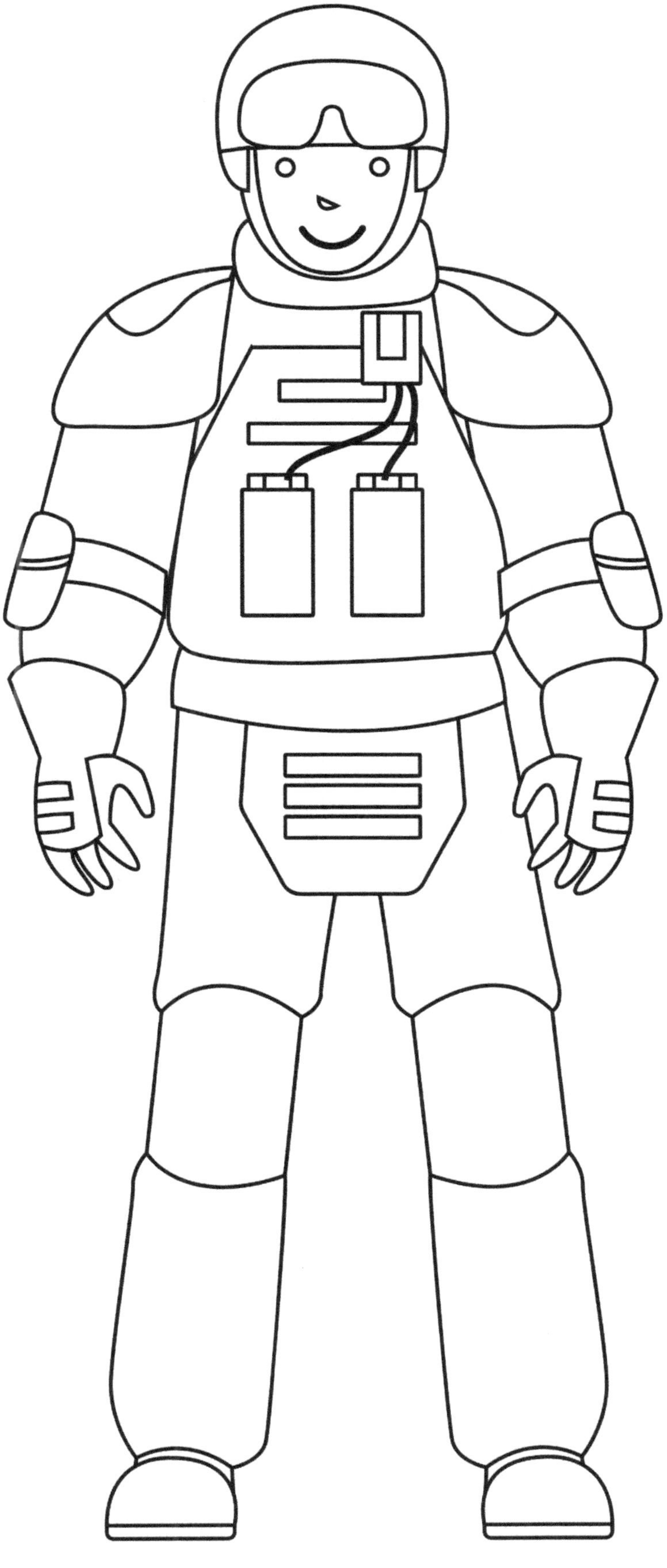

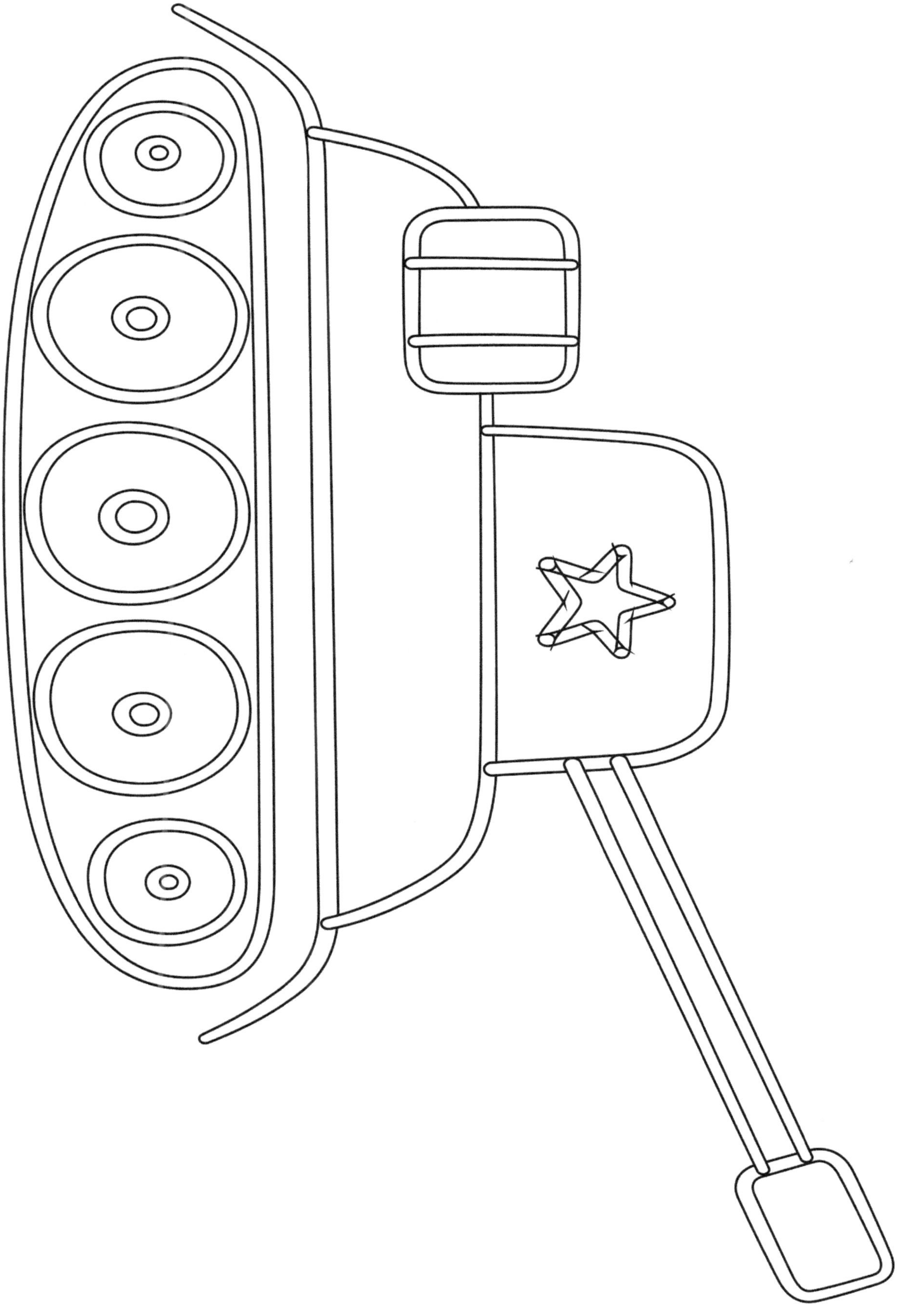

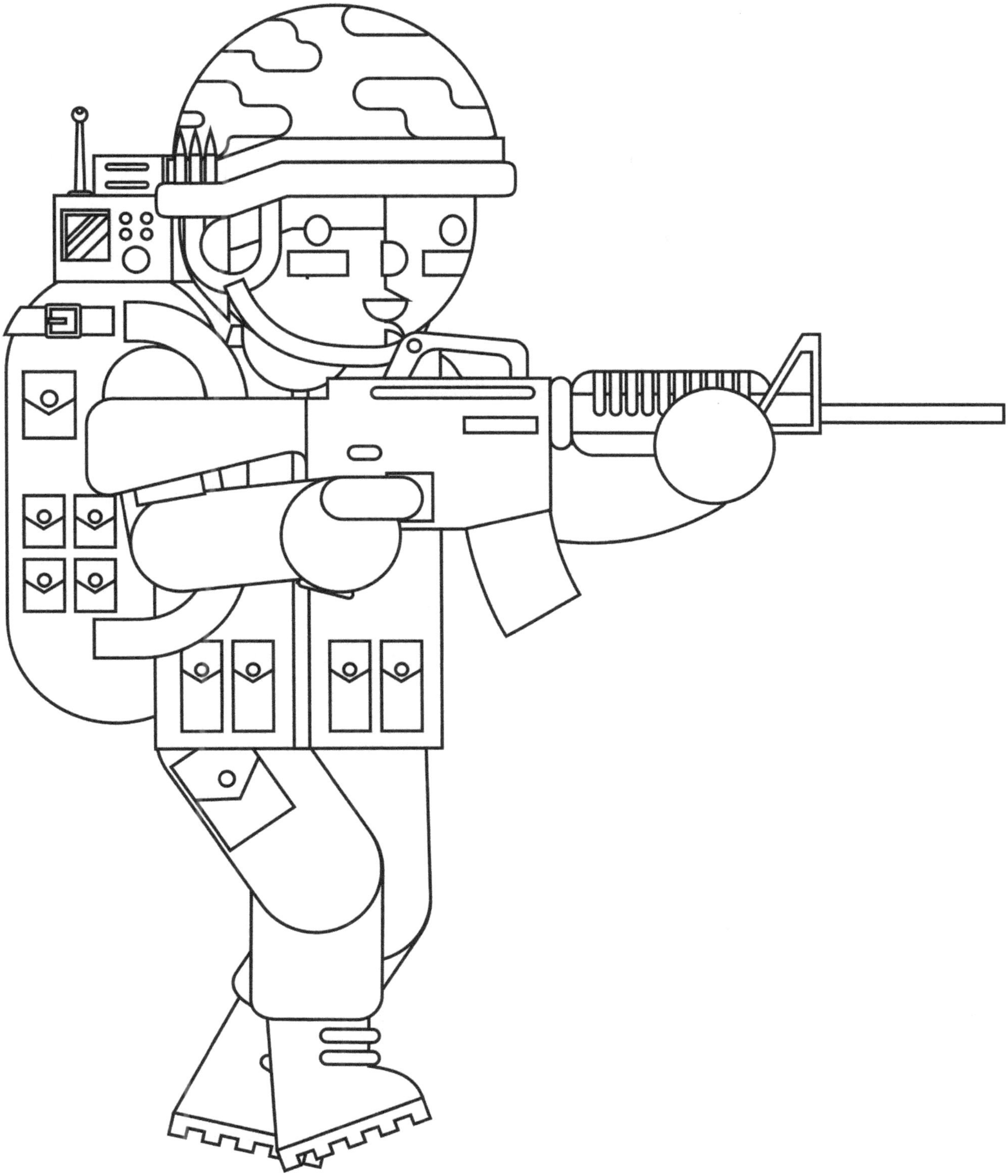

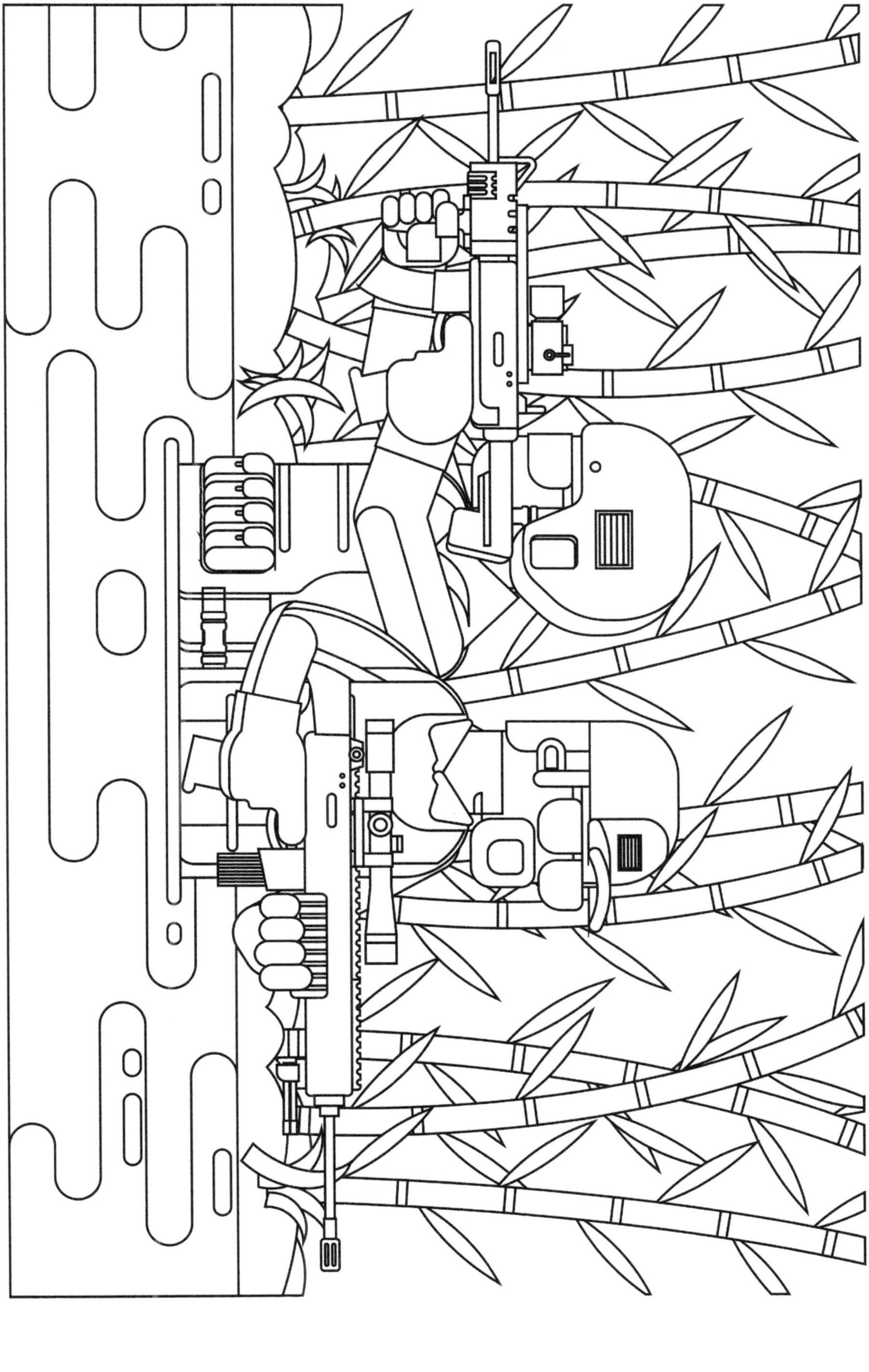

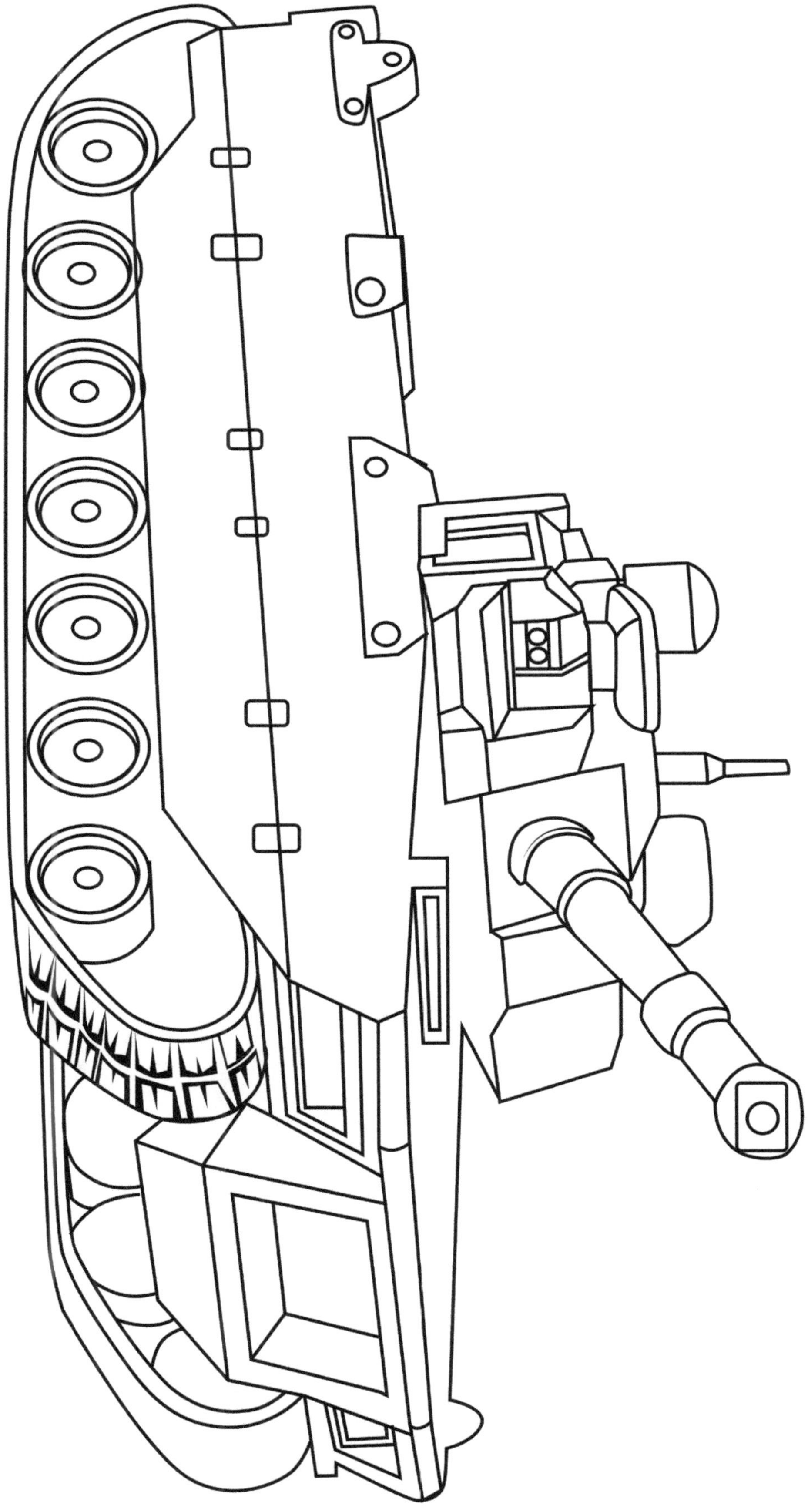

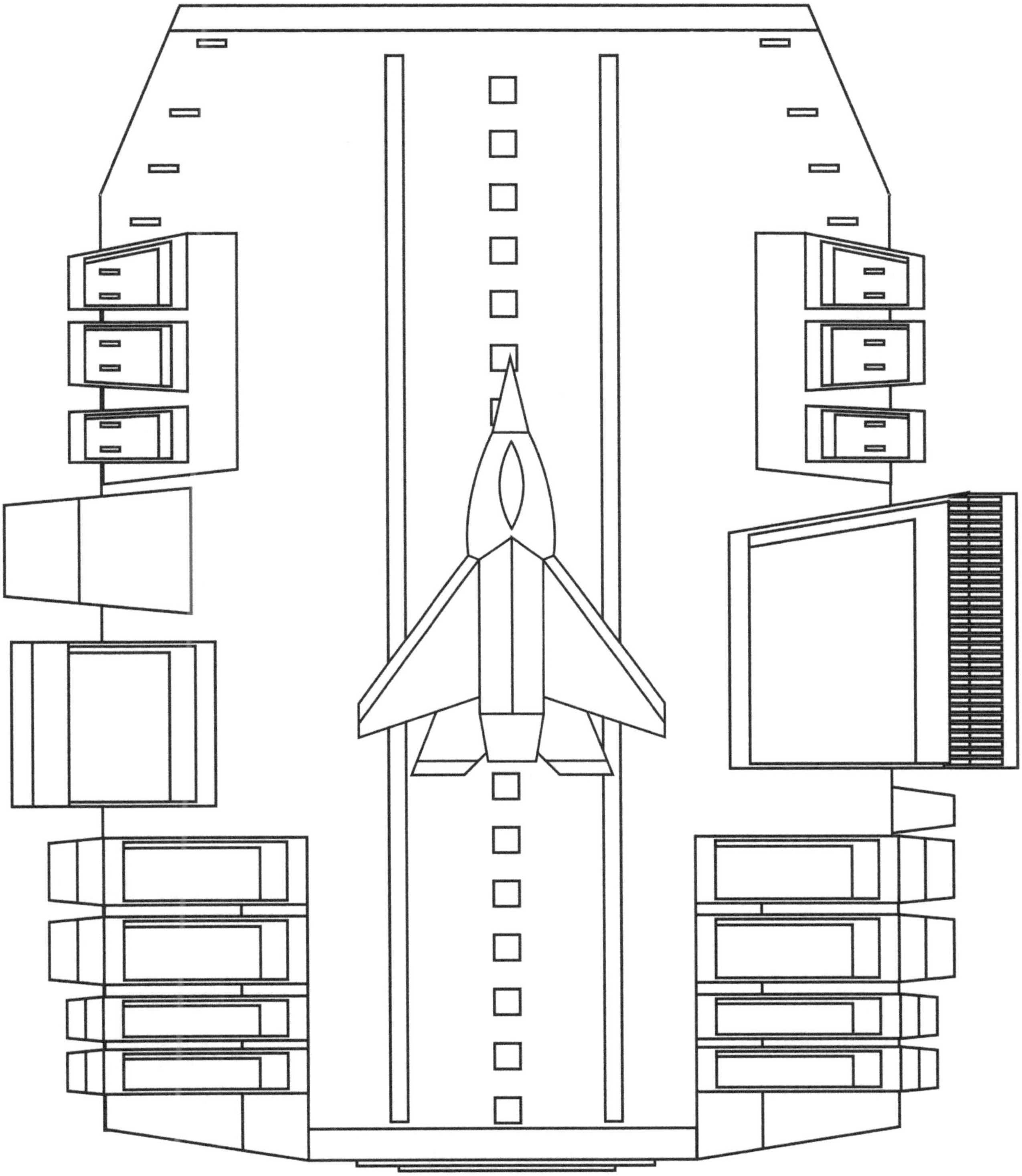

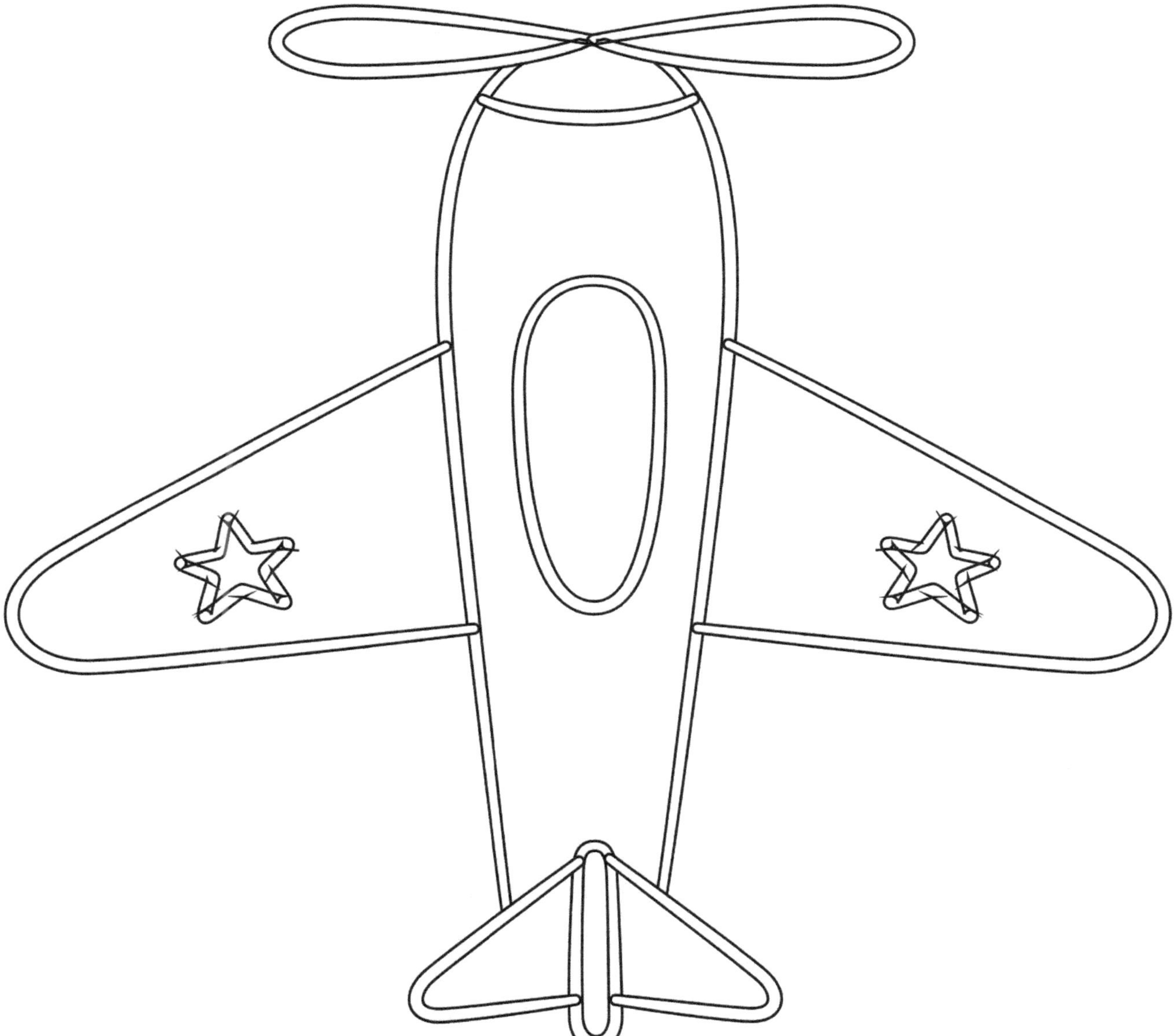

AIRBASE

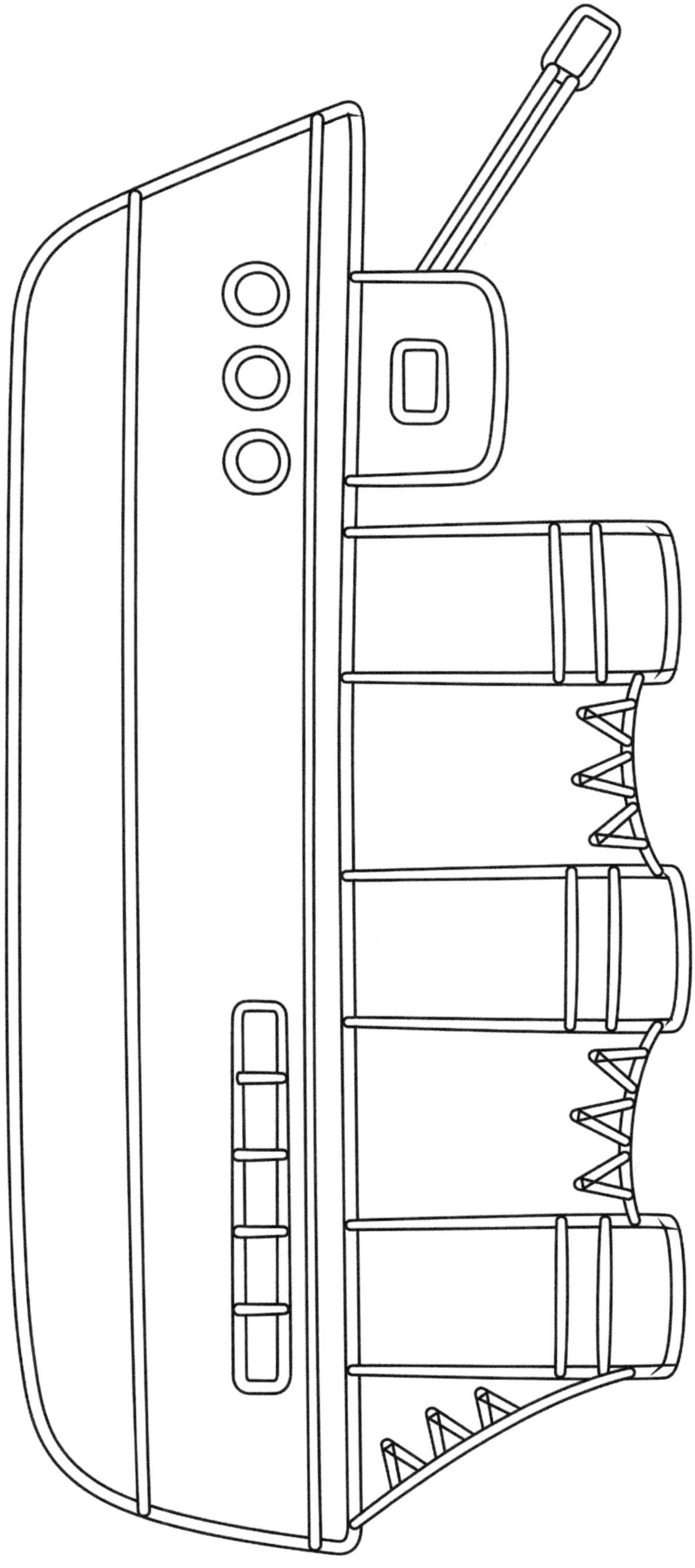

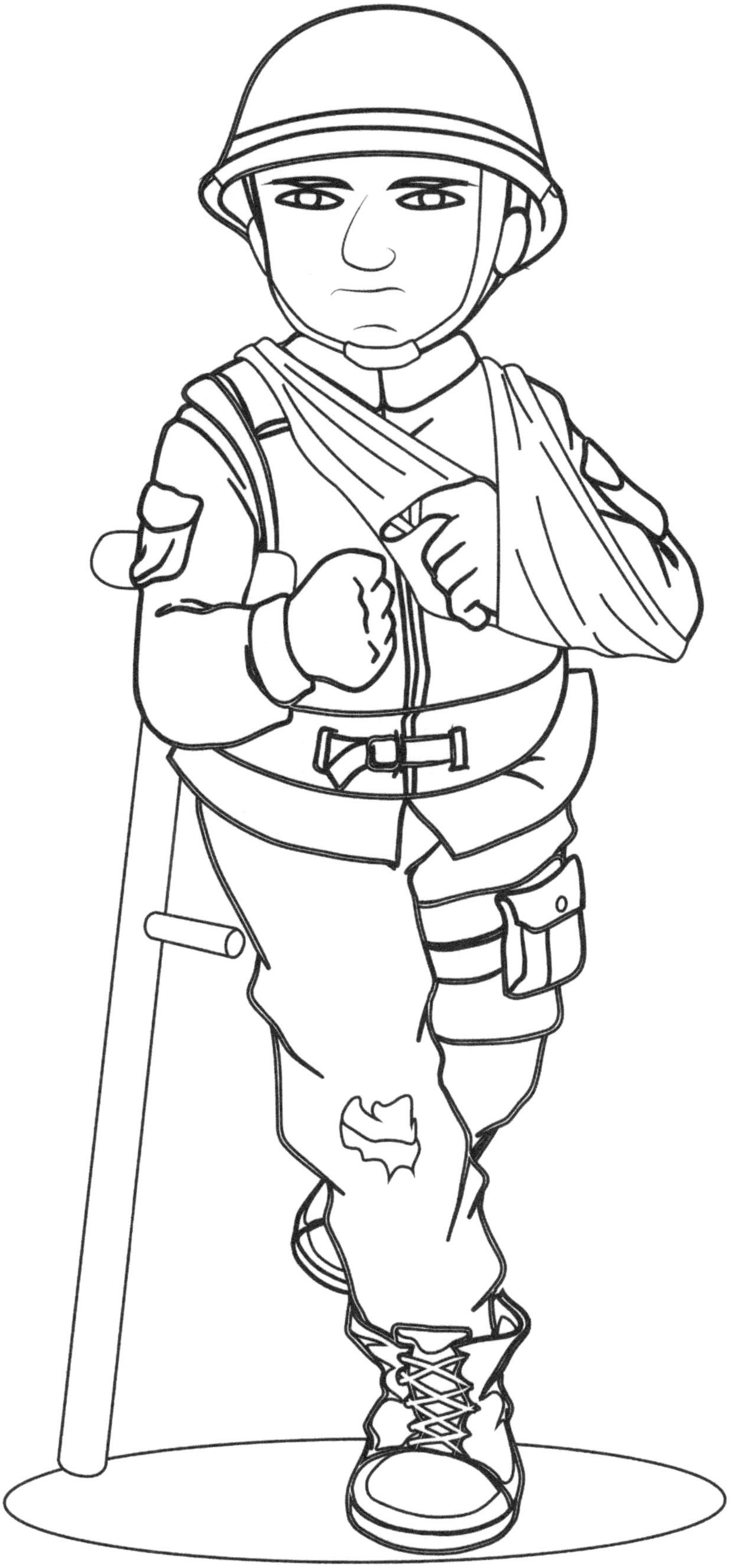

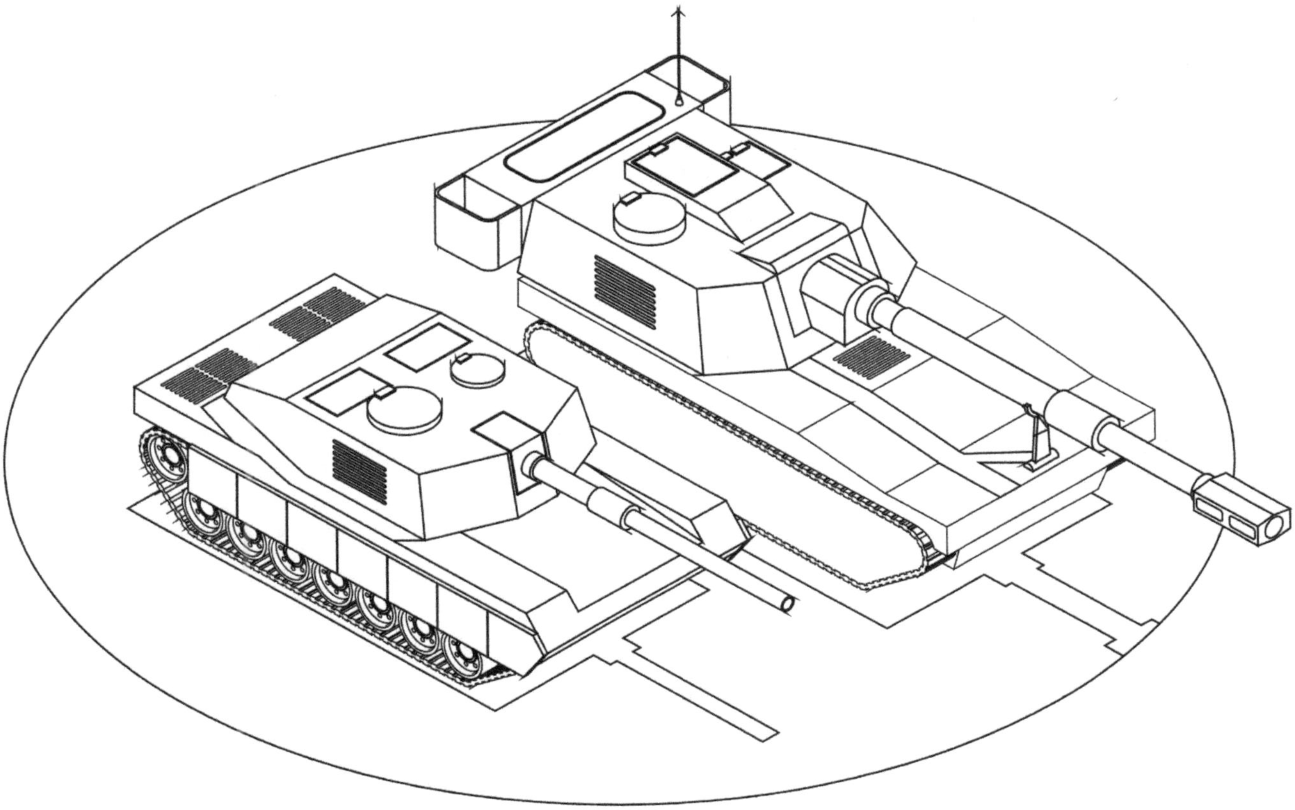

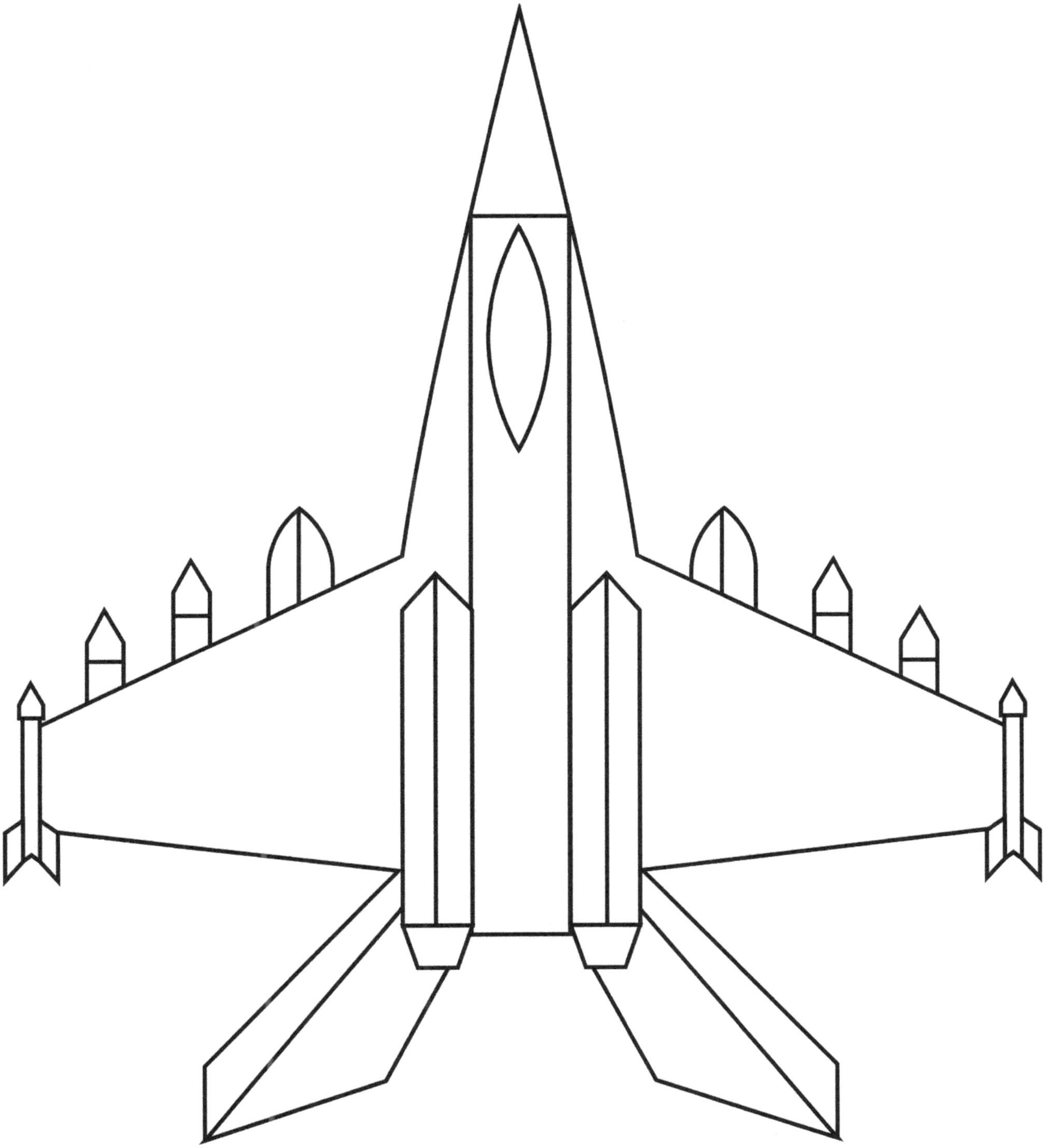

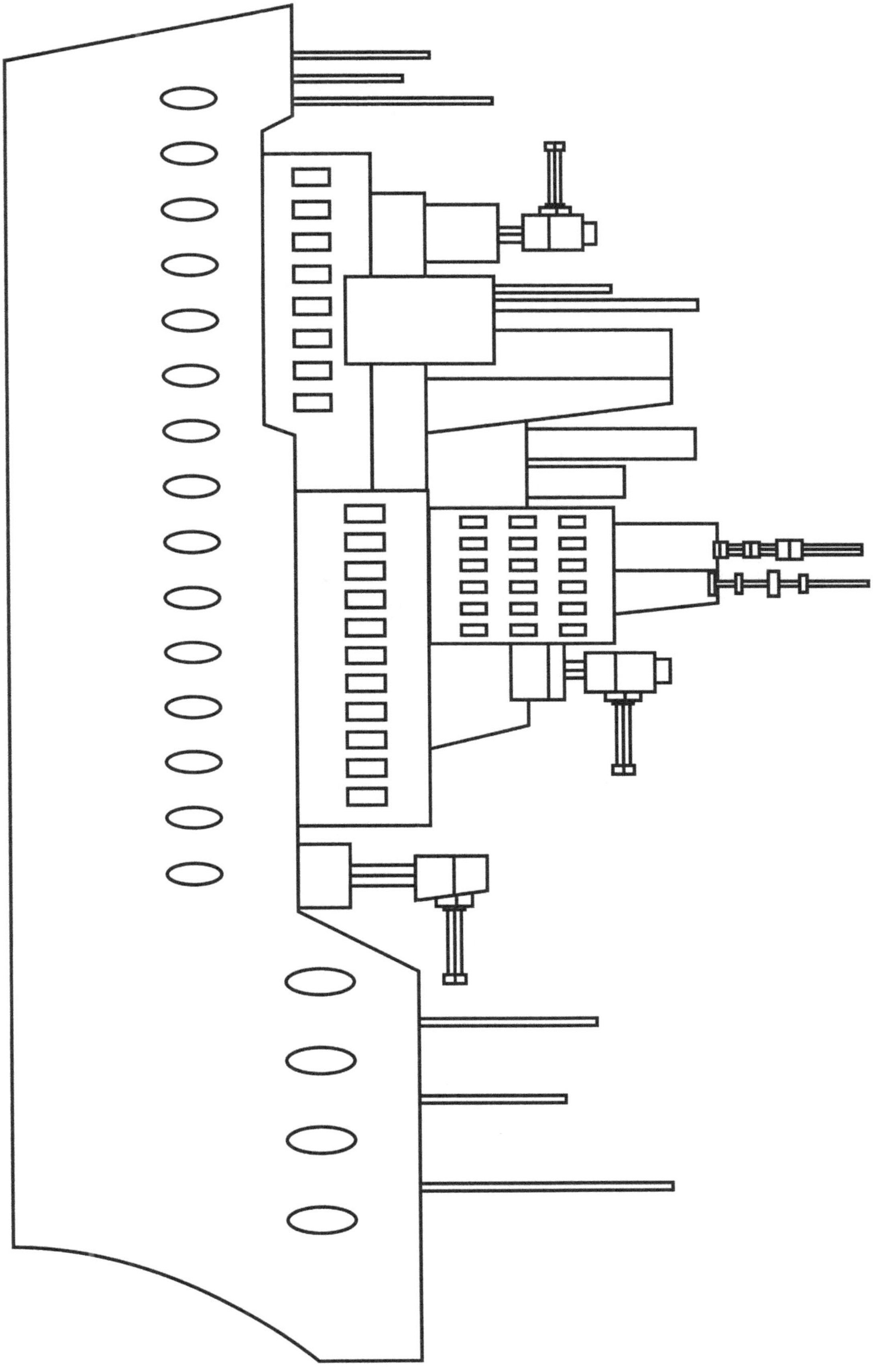

Printed in the USA
CPSIA information can be obtained
at www.ICGtesting.com
LVHW082151031224
798267LV00046B/2159
* 9 7 9 8 7 2 1 0 0 1 6 5 9 *